How to Keep Your Stuff Safe Online

Raef Meeuwisse

Cyber Simplicity Ltd, Hythe, KENT, UK.   CT21 5HE.

Email:	orders@cybersimplicity.com
Twitter:	@RaefMeeuwisse
First Edition:	8 March 2017
Published by:	Cyber Simplicity Ltd

www.cybersimplicity.com

www.howtokeepyourstuffsafeonline.com

Ordering Information:

Special discounts are available on quantity purchases by corporations, associations, educators, and others. For details, contact the publisher at the above listed address.

Trade and wholesalers: Please contact Cyber Simplicity Ltd.

Tel/Fax: +44(0)1227 540 540

ISBN-13:	978-1-911452-17-1 (p)
ISBN-13:	978-1-911452-18-8 (e)

DEDICATION

My thanks to Christine Cavalier (@PurpleCar) for suggesting I create something more accessible for the mainstream and to Giles Turnbull (@GilesT) for the book title idea. Feel free to tweet me improvement ideas @RaefMeeuwisse

What happens online, does not always stay online.

Disclaimer:

This publication is designed to provide very basic, general guidance that (if followed) can help as part of your approach to reduce the risk of being compromised by a cyber attack. Security is never impenetrable. Risks, threats and controls are constantly evolving. This book is for guidance only and no warranty or guarantee is inferred or implied.

Also Available

Also available from this author in paperback & digital formats:

The Encrypted Pocketbook of Passwords
Writing down your passwords is usually fraught with risks. The Encrypted Pocketbook of Passwords helps you to store your passwords more securely in a format that you can read but that others will find hard to break.

The Cybersecurity to English Dictionary
All of the primary cybersecurity terminology translated into everyday English definitions.

Cybersecurity for Beginners
This book provides an easy insight into the full discipline of cybersecurity, even if you have a non-technical background.

Cybersecurity Exposed: The Cyber House Rules
Explores the causes for the increased magnitude and frequency of cybercrime. Why is cybersecurity frequently left vulnerable to attack? Is there a set of principles that can be applied to help correct the problems?

Cybersecurity: Home and Small Business
Guidance on the basic security practices we can apply at home or in small businesses to help decrease the risk of being successfully attacked.

Visit www.cybersimplicity.com for a full list of the latest titles.

Looking for great corporate promotional gifts?
Check out our offers at www.cybersimplicity.com

Raef Meeuwisse

CONTENTS

INTRODUCTION

Cybercrime has become a pandemic. It is the fastest growing industry in the world and has in the past few years become the main form of crime in almost all countries.

Often, we are given the misleading impression that defending against these threats is nearly impossible. That is not true. It is actually relatively simple to take a number of basic defensive steps that will massively reduce your chances of being scammed, conned or compromised.

Although I already write a more comprehensive publication (Cybersecurity: Home and Small Business), the objective for this publication is to write something much more compact and accessible for the everyday person who just wants to know the very basics of keeping themselves safe online.

So buckle up and stand by for some fast, furious and basic measures that if you implement them can take your risk of online compromise down to just a few percent.

With so many people managing their personal, online security very badly – and a large number of organizations in a similar position, cyber criminals have a vast oasis of targets to choose from.

To take the old story of the two men being chased by a bear;

The slower man says 'Stop running, you will never outrun the bear.'

The other man responds, 'I don't need to outrun the bear. I only need to outrun you.

You don't have to have perfect security to avoid being compromised. You only need to have better security than most people.

Raef Meeuwisse

How to Keep Your Stuff Safe Online

Cyber Attack Basics:

Criminals
seek
vulnerabilities (security gaps)
to
exploit (take advantage of)
for
financial or political gain.

Where am I Vulnerable?

If you look at how cyber criminals operate, they have 3 basic tactics:

1) To get your credentials for an online service, so they can log-in and cause harm.

2) To install malicious software on any device you own that connects to the Internet, so they can log-in and cause harm.

3) To perform a confidence trick on you, to get you to do something with your valid access.

In each of these tactics, the harm or end goal for the criminal can be to steal your money, steal your information, ransom the content back to you or even to post content that can negatively impact you.

The Internet is like the world wild west. Sending and receiving any information over the Internet is somewhat similar to travelling through unsafe territory. Your journey will only be as safe as the precautions you choose to take.

Here are some examples of the tactics that are used:

A credential attack:

Jimmy had so many passwords to remember, he often re-used the same one across many different online services. The criminals managed to break into the servers at one of his online services. They stole and decrypted all of the username and password details and then used automated tools to work out where else those same details worked. They were able to sell his log-in details to other criminals. All of the accounts he was using with those details began to experience fraud.

A malware attack:

Frank was just surfing a link from a search engine on a topic of interest. He didn't notice anything wrong with the page he went to but because he was running out of date software and ineffective anti-malware, he unknowingly installed some malware. A day later, his screen froze with a ransomware demand for money to release his device.

A confidence trick:

Janet was buying a house. She received an email that appeared to come from her lawyer with a change of bank details for the balance transfer. After the transfer was made, it turned out that the email was a fraud.

Getting safe online requires looking at personal security from these 3 different angles.

1) How to select and protect your online services.

2) How to better protect you internet connected devices.

3) How to be alert to confidence tricks.

This book is therefore arranged into three main sections:

- Securing Online Services

- Securing Digital Devices

- Avoiding Scams

There are also 2 further sections that provide information that cover how you can take your online anonymity further and an abridged set of definitions taken from another of my publications, **The Cybersecurity to English Dictionary**.

This book is intentionally brief, to set out simple but effective defensive measures that can be taken, mostly at no cost. It is designed to provide the main security steps that can be read and implemented rapidly. If you implement all the steps, your security will not be perfect but it should be good enough to avoid 99% of threats.

Securing Online Services

Banking, shopping, social media, email, on demand TV and even tax returns, almost everything is now looking for us to subscribe to an online service.

Disturbingly, even the organizations running these services are frequently unable to prevent security intrusions.

It can *seem* that securing our individual online accounts would be difficult. In fact, it is far more straightforward. After all, if an organization is compromised that should always be their responsibility.

As private individuals, what we need to do is be responsible enough to ensure that we are not individually susceptible to a cyber attack.

So these are the steps to help secure your own personal online world.

Passwords

Almost every service seems to want us to set-up a separate username and password. Often the username is required to be our email address.

The problem is that most people now manage as many as 100 passwords or more.

Cyber criminals know that statistically, over 70% of us re-use five passwords or less across all of our online accounts. They harvest passwords from services that have been breached and then use automated tools to see what other services they will unlock.

For that reason, it is essential to **use a separate unique and strong password on each different online account of value.**

However, to do that you need a safe way to record and access the passwords, otherwise even you will not be able to get in!

I am not an advocate of online password managers. After all, because they are online, they themselves can be compromised (and several services have had this issue).

So what can you do?

My own solution was to create 'The Encrypted Pocketbook of Passwords', available on Amazon and via good bookshops. It is a physical password journal that uses secret keys so that even if the book is stolen, the thief would still be unable to guess your passwords, unless they know your secret keys.

However, you don't need to buy that book. The key messages in that book are:

- Each account of any value must have a unique and separate password.

- It is okay to write most of each password down, as long as you don't write out enough of each one that the missing piece can be guessed.

- You also need to keep any written information as secure as possible.

I recommend something physical (pen and paper) rather than electronic for this reason: *Most attacks will be from overseas and any physical theft would be local.*

You should also be aware that most thieves know that passwords are usually written down and kept within 3 feet of the device used to access the services – so keep any physical journal as hidden as possible.

I also recommend keeping 2 journals, so if one is stolen or

mislaid, the back-up can be used to recover and change them.

Another tip for passwords is that statisticians have worked out (based on cracking passwords) that long passwords that used random words was stronger than using 8-12 characters with lots of random characters.

!@fgh5yr as a password could be cracked within a few minutes.

Lambsevensquidfortypurpleepsilon as a password would take days or even weeks to crack (as at early 2017) due to its length. If you add in some special characters and numbers too – it takes even longer to crack.

Although you might not want to set long passwords on every online account, it is worth going to that effort on the accounts that could have the highest value and impact if they were compromised. If, for example, an account has the ability to make any kind of payment or contains information that is sensitive or of high value – make sure you set a long and unique password with at least 13 characters.

Multi-factor authentication

Passwords alone are no longer considered by the security community to offer an adequate level of security, especially if the online service is handling any information or transactions of value.

Before choosing to use any online service, look to see if they have something called **two-factor authentication** or **multi-factor authentication**. What this means in simple English is that access is not only reliant on knowing the username and password, it will also require proof through something you have (for example by sending a code in a text to your verified phone) or something you are (voice recognition, face recognition or other biometric confirmation).

If an online service offers multi-factor authentication and you want to keep it secure, enable and use this function. Twitter, PayPal and thousands of other services offer this capability.

For example, my twitter account will not let any new device log-in, even if the credentials are accurate unless I verify my identity through a code that is texted to my phone and then re-entered on the site.

Phone verification also alerts you to any unauthorized access attempts because you will receive an unexpected text.

Although there are some emergent scams that can get around these measures, they make life much harder for any attack. Unless you are of special interest, multi-factor authentication will often be enough to persuade the attacker to move on to another target.

Privacy and security settings

All applications like to gather and share as much information about their subscribers as possible. After all, the more they know about you, the more they can monetize that information.

Sadly, cybercriminals can also gather a lot of information through both the information you allow to be publicly accessible and information they may steal from service providers.

There are also usually a number of security and privacy settings that you can select to increase your online safety. Remarkably, most people do not set these options at the level they would if they stopped to research and configure them.

For example, within most operating systems, including Windows 10, there are a number of privacy settings that can prevent sharing information about your browsing and usage patterns. If you select the 'express' set-up option, you normally bypass all of the options and permit the manufacturer to better target advertising and promotions. (You can always change these settings and find out how using Google and YouTube).

In addition, there are nearly always additional security settings that can be applied, for example:

- On Twitter you can set up secondary authentication via a phone to require a code before any new device with the right username and password can access your account.

- PayPal has a similar feature, requiring a code before any transfer is made.

You can often also check what devices are currently authorized to use your account and block any that should no longer be permitted.

So remember to check what security options are available on any online service of value that you choose to use – and apply the strongest settings you are happy to use.

For example, do you really want your LinkedIn or Facebook profile to be public? It's relatively easy to restrict who can view them.

Appropriate use

It is a sensible suggestion to consider carefully what information you choose to put into any online service, even if you think it is secure; there are still several ways that the information may eventually become exposed.

So remember to think carefully about what information you choose to place into any online service. The users of an online infidelity service found out the hard way that their confidential details do not always stay confidential.

Unlike Vegas, what happens online frequently stays online.

Remember that social media and alcohol rarely mix. Avoid using social media platforms or posting photos online if or when you are intoxicated.

Service history

If you know a service provider has suffered from a number of public breaches, it is a safe bet that they have considerable security issues.

You may think those issues would be resolved. In fact, they tend to be a symptom that the provider is not very good at fixing them.

When selecting a service provider, such as a bank, a password manager or even a file sharing service, select with care. Aim to use a decent size service provider, because they can normally afford better security and also one that has suffered only the most minor of security issues.

Using safe connections

Intercepting online communications is still often used to steal money and information.

Some criminals even go so far as to set-up public, free, Wi-Fi connections in busy target areas, so they can either steal copies of the information used over the connection, or even perform 'man-in-the-middle' style attacks where they provide fake sites that look real so they can hijack what you think is a real online banking session.

An insecure connection can also be used to enter your device if you do not have great security software installed, or if you are running an out of date version of your operating system. (That's one of the reasons Donald Trump got criticism for using a 3 year old smartphone).

Take care to keep your sensitive online transactions and logging in activities to secure connections. As a general rule, it is unwise to use free Wi-Fi for banking and other high value transactions you care about.

If you do frequently need to use public Wi-Fi, you can subscribe to a VPN (virtual private network) service, although again – make sure it is with a known and trusted service. If the service is free or not very well known, it may also be used to steal your information.

Many browsers will also show a red bar in the internet address line at the top if it detects a security problem. Although seeing a green line is not always an assurance that the site really is safe, a red background on the top line is definitely a sign that the site and service is not secure and should not be used.

Encryption

For any online service where you are storing files that you consider to be sensitive in any way, make sure you find out what the encryption options are – and apply them appropriately.

If there are no 'built-in' encryption options, you can look to encrypt files yourself before you upload them.

What encryption does is to convert something readable (to cipher it) into something that is not readable unless you have the correct 'key' to unlock and view it.

If I store a copy of documents and images that are encrypted, anyone who accesses them without the key would not be able to read them unless they could break the encryption, or obtain a copy of the decryption key.

Back-up

Two words. *Contingency option.*

If you want a contingency option in the event that your online account becomes sabotaged or unavailable, remember to keep a copy (a back-up) of the information some place accessible. You also need to ensure that wherever you store your copies has appropriate security.

Most security professionals look to ensure their back-ups have at least the same level of security in place as the main information they are using day to day.

This topic (how to achieve a good back-up regime) is covered further later in the book.

Only use secure devices

Although it can seem convenient to use any device to connect to an online service, remember that if the device itself is not secure, it can bypass all of your other good security efforts.

If you do need to go online from an untrusted device, perhaps a public terminal at an airport, be sure to change your password as soon as you can get back to using a secure device. Your service will be at risk until you do.

Delete dead accounts and information

If you stop using a particular online service, they are usually obliged to offer you the option to fully and permanently delete the account.

It is worthwhile deleting any accounts that you no longer need. Leaving inactive accounts in place can often lead to problems if someone else gains access and starts to use it for unauthorized objectives.

As an example, they might be able to use that account to pretend to be you and open other online services in your name.

Limit credit cards

Another useful but non-technical tip is to be very careful about what credit cards or accounts you link to any online service.

If you do have to attach a payment method to an account, it is highly advisable to ensure that it has strict financial limits. For example – I might be able to use a pre-paid credit card that has no ability to overspend its balance. In that way, it would be hard for any transaction that tried to break the limit to be justified. In the event that a payment broke the payment limit, it should be automatically declined. If your provider refuses to block payments that exceed your credit limit – I would definitely advise switching provider to one that does.

So remember – being safe with your online services is all about taking these simple steps;

- Use a unique password

- Make the password strong and long

- Enable a secondary form of authentication where it is available

- Set the strongest privacy and security options in each service that you feel comfortable with

- Use your online services appropriately and avoid

placing compromising material online

- Look to only use online services that are established (have a large number of users) and no back history of multiple major security breaches.

- Be careful about what internet connections you use.

- Be careful to stick to trusted, secure devices (see the next section for device security)

- Encrypt any sensitive information that you allow online

- Take a copy of any critical or important information and store it securely away from the main service.

- Choose to completely delete any online accounts that you no longer have a use for.

Securing Digital Devices

I can tell you that the idea that it is really difficult to make most of your devices secure is hogwash. It requires only a few basic steps to help prevent most intrusions happening – but these are steps that very few people currently take.

There are a few exceptions, if you are running a very old device that is no longer able to receive security updates, or an operating system that is no longer supported, your device will have gaps that can be taken advantage of.

That said, even with an out of date device, applying these steps will still be far more secure than using a similar device that does not apply them.

Controlling installation privileges

One of the most frequent security gaps the majority of private people have is that they run their devices from an account where they can also install new software. After all, if you own the device, it can seem to make sense to run the device from an account that has this power. However, you will be more protected if you have an additional account (an administrative account with a password), separate from your everyday usage account.

The majority of malware (malicious software) is unable to install itself if you are not logged in with administrative permission.

If you follow these simple steps, you can transfer the installation permission to a separate administrative account. If most types of malware try to get in, you will get an unexpected prompt asking you to enter your administrators password (don't do it!) In this simple way, you will have prevented installing quite a high percentage of attempts to install unwanted or malicious software.

- Login to your device as normal.

- Go to users and settings.

- Setup a new user and give that new user full administrative permission.

- Be sure to set a password on the new account (a password you can remember as you may use it infrequently)

- Logout

- Login to the new account

- Downgrade the account you use on a day-to-day basis so that it only has standard permissions (no permission to install new software)

This simple measure will substantially enhance your security. Nothing can now install without prompting you for a password, unless the malware itself knows how to bypass this security measure – and most of them cannot.

Updating software (patch management)

Nearly all malware works by taking advantage of known gaps in operating systems and other software (security people call these *vulnerabilities* that can be *exploited*).

If you keep your devices (smartphones, laptops, computers,…) up to date with the very latest updates from their manufacturers, you will increase your device security at least ten-fold compared to a device that has not taken this step.

Remember though, that if your device or its operating system, or other software is no longer supported (meaning the manufacturer is no longer providing updates), then that will still mean that your device has security gaps.

Installing effective anti-malware

The majority of cybercrime relies on installing malicious software (**malware**) on their victims' device. That device could be anything you connect to the Internet. It could be a laptop, a smartphone, a tablet or other 'smart' device.

Although there are many anti-malware (also sometimes called endpoint security) software options, many of them, including some of the most well known are actually not very effective.

Some of the latest 'nextgen' endpoint security solutions (Cylance is one product – but there are also others) can detect and block the majority of malware where other products will not.

Look for a product that claims to be >99% effective at detecting and blocking all types of malware. Usually this kind of solution will explain that it works using a basic form of artificial intelligence called 'machine learning' to identify and block malicious threats, even if it has no prior exposure to that threat. It will recognize most malicious threats simply by recognizing patterns and behaviors, even if the file has never been opened.

As an example, corporate environments with ineffective anti-malware are constantly run off their feet resolving and cleaning problems. Conversely, environments using the newer (at present less well known and slightly more expensive) nextgen solutions suffer a small fraction of those issues.

It is worth taking the time to research the best anti-malware solution – and to use something like Cylance as a benchmark. They can be purchased for home use – but in 2017 – you have to look to find them as they mostly sell to corporate customers.

Device firewall

A device firewall is like a digital brick wall. The only electronic information that can pass through has to meet certain tests and checks.

Many operating systems and devices have device firewalls included as standard. This security technology is also often included with many of the anti-malware solutions.

The key step is to check if your device has a firewall and to make sure it is turned on.

As there are so many different devices, the simplest way to check is to Google your operating system with the word 'firewall' and find out what the options are. For example, Windows includes Windows Defender as standard, which includes a firewall feature and there are also additional enhanced firewall products available.

Removing default accounts

Some items that can connect to the Internet, especially routers, CCTV devices and 'smart' Internet of Things items often come with an in initial username and password preset. If that is the case, you should aim to replace and change the password, and if possible, the default username as soon as possible. This should preferably be the very first time you use the device.

One of the first things that a cyber attacker will often look for is any default accounts – as the username is often 'admin' (or similar) and the password is sometimes also a standard default value. If they can access that account, they will be able to use it in various ways, consuming your Internet bandwidth and potentially using it as an access point to any other nearby devices.

As an example, in 2016, a huge amount of service disruption attacks (known as distributed denial of service or DDoS attacks) were performed by leveraging Internet of Things devices such as connected CCTV boxes that had been shipped with default usernames and passwords.

Security & privacy settings

Things as simple as setting a password on your device to logon can improve your device security. As separately covered, ensuring the device has a firewall in place and an effective anti-malware solution in place also make a substantial difference.

You may also find other security features that are available on your device. For example, it may be possible to enable encryption, so that if your smartphone, laptop or whatever it happens to be is stolen, the information can only be retrieved if they can break through the password.

It is always worth checking what security options your particular device offers and setting them to the highest level you feel comfortable with.

Just like with online services, the manufacturer of your device and any software that is installed will also want to collect as much information about you as possible. They should obtain your permission to do that – but often they bundle that permission in with an incredibly long, initial consent agreement.

Remember to be careful to pay attention to privacy settings. As previously mentioned, even operating systems like Windows will have privacy options that you can configure to prevent having information about your usage and web browsing used to target you for advertising.

You can usually discover what privacy options are available by Googling your device name, together with the words 'privacy settings'.

Pay attention during any software installation to what permissions are being requested. If a software installation is requesting excessive permissions, it is usually better not to install it.

Install only trusted software

Another way of compromising your online accounts is simply by getting you to install software that has hidden and malicious functionality.

That 'free' PDF creator or other software may not be as low cost as you think, especially if it contains functions that can spy on your usage and steal information, including your login details to online services.

Even some humble smartphone 'torch' applications have been found to take personal information, such as contact details.

Install only what you need - and check out the legitimacy of any unknown software _before_ installing it. You can often check if the software by simply Googling the name of the software plus the word 'malware' to find out if anyone has experienced issues with it.

Controlling device usage

Remember that allowing another person to use one or more of your devices, opens up the potential for them to accidentally (or otherwise) expose it to malware.

Take care to only let people use access where they have no installation privileges. You should also only let people use your device if you fully trust that they will not be visiting exotic sites that may be full of malware!

Securing connections (USBs & routers)

USB devices are a great way for malware infections to spread. If a USB device has been plugged into a device with an infection, it is usually able to transfer that infection to other devices it is attached to.

Sharing USB devices is often likened to sharing needles. Be careful that you only use USB devices, especially memory sticks, between devices that have trusted levels of security.

Having weak security on your own home Internet connection is also another potential way-in for an attacker.

Setup the strongest key for your wireless internet connection. At least 20 characters long is a good idea, especially if you live in a city or other crowded area where you might get more drive-by attempts to access your home connection.

WI-FI is not regarded as incredibly secure, but some connection types are stronger than others. Look at what options your router provide and opt for the strongest security option you can use. WPA2 is considered more secure than WEP – but there are sometimes even more robust connection options available.

Routers also typically have default passwords and need to be logged into to check for and install security software updates. Remember to login to your router at initial install and then on a regular basis to check for and install any updates.

There is also a great, FREE resource available on the Internet that can check whether your router has any basic, wide open issues: https://www.grc.com/shieldsup (link valid as at March 2017).

Avoid networking devices

Due to the increase in the amount of malware infection rates, it is no longer a good idea to choose to provide trusted access by default across devices.

With cloud services now available, there are often options that will allow you to collaborate between devices without giving them permission to directly access each other.

As an example, in a small household or small business where there are 4 or 5 devices, if they are networked, an infection can impact all of the devices. If they are not, only the device that is initially infected should be impacted.

Similarly, remember that a 'shared' device, such as a network storage device can also become a transmission point for any infection.

A network storage device (see **NAS** [network attached storage] in the dictionary section) is a physical device that can be attached to a network so that you can send or share files between different devices. They are great for sharing music, video, photos – but they can also spread infections. If you rely *only* on a NAS to back-up your data, you can often find that your back-up is also compromised.

Backing up data

Ransomware is still on the rise. This is a form of malware that demands payment before it will release your device or files back to you.

With all of the other security measures outlined in this brief book in place, your risk from ransomware is reduced but not completely eliminated.

However, if you have a protected copy (a back-up) of your information, you will be able to recover your information without giving in to any criminal demands.

If you really want to keep a copy of your valuable information safe, it is advisable to follow the 3/2/1 rule:

- Keep **3** copies of the data.

- Store them on at least **2** different formats (for example, on an encrypted USB stick and in an encrypted online storage service)

- Make sure at least **1** of the copies is kept offsite.

It is important to note that if you get malware on a device, then attach something (like a USB stick) to it – you are almost certain to spread the problem to the connected device.

Never keep your back-up storage connected to the devices they are designed to protect. If you do that, rather than keeping a safe copy of your files, you can find that your back-up information is also lost in the event of a problem.

Email and messaging is not secure

It is possible to add encryption to email and messaging platforms. However, it is essential to understand that when you send out any message, you are immediately at the mercy of the recipient/s of your message.

Even if you spend a lot of time and money on message security, all of your effort can be undone by the security or actions of any recipient.

If you want to keep your messages safe during transmission, you can implement encryption on your email or messaging service. That should keep it reasonably secure during transmission – but the security will not be under your control once it gets to an authorized recipient.

So my guidance here is 2 fold:

1) Treat any message you trust to a recipient as something that you cannot keep safe.

2) If you are sending any sensitive information, look to install or configure encryption on your email. This is a purchasable product on some platforms and there are also free versions that can be installed. It will help to keep the information safe until it reaches the recipient.

Keep in mind the number of news stories that involved a celebrity sending out an inadvisable opinion via email, text or other messaging service. These were usually leaked due to the security or actions of the recipient rather than the sender.

Avoiding Scams

Ultimately, the easiest and weakest point for any cyber criminal to attack to achieve financial gain is the user with the legitimate access to devices and accounts.

You could have completely impenetrable security from a technology perspective – but that technology is still required to let you – the legitimate user, instruct it to do things.

Criminals know this and have multiple types of ploys and scams to try and get you to reveal information about your access (such as revealing your password) or they can simply try to get you to unwittingly make a transaction based on false information.

Many of these scams are just like the confidence tricks of old – so remember – if something seems too good to be true – it probably is.

These are just some of the tactics that are used – so remember to always be on guard for people that are trying to get you to reveal private information, click on unknown links or make quick transactions due to time pressure.

Scam emails and websites (phishing)

The term *phishing* is the technical term used to describe the cybercrime technique to get you to release information or unintended access to something you actually want to keep secure.

The sophistication of the techniques used varies. Some scams are very easy to spot and some are much harder to recognize.

At the most basic level, if you receive an unsolicited

communication (something you were not expecting or did not ask for) – you should always consider the communication with suspicion.

As an example, web services such as PayPal will never email you a link asking you to confirm your password via a link that appears to go to their website. That is a very frequent type of phishing technique.

You should always treat links or requests for information with suspicion and if you really believe that they are genuine, seek to verify their authenticity away from that communication. For example, if a communication appears to come from a site you subscribe to – manually go to the website (not via any link in the email) and contact their support desk, helpdesk or fraud line to verify if the communication is genuine.

If in any doubt – do not proceed.

You also need to be very careful not to open any attachments to any email, message or even over the Internet IF you have any doubts about that files authenticity.

When a cyber criminal attempts a phishing scam, they are usually hoping for one or both of the following to happen:

- To get you to reveal some secret information.

- To get you to install some malicious software without even realizing it has happened.

Even opening a simple document (PDF or Word) can be enough to install malicious software against your will.

If you have followed the other guidance in this book (for example - no installation privileges, up to date software and nextgen anti-malware), you may still be protected from malware if this happens – but it is far better not to take that chance.

Remember also that a phishing scam usually tries to intentionally panic you into rapid action. I receive hundreds of alleged security alerts by email and so far, not one of them has been genuine. However, each alert will seek to panic me into believing that my account or funds are at risk unless I take the action they outline in their message.

It may be that they want me to call a telephone number (that turns out to be a premium rate number), visit a website (that would then try to install malware), or open a spreadsheet or other document to confirm the contents (that would also try to install malware).

More sophisticated scams will often use some real information to help with their confidence trick. They may have obtained some information about you – for example, your name, 4 digits from your credit card and/or the fact you subscribe to a particular web service. Do not take the fact that any message you did not ask for contains some real information as any proof that the message itself is genuine.

Not all phishing happens through email. It is also possible that if you are looking for something on the Internet, a search result or link in one page can take you to an unsafe Internet location that will try to install malware.

Only download files or install applications from sites and services that you are sure are safe.

There are also some security services you can install that will help guard against many of the unsafe Internet locations, however, although these can help, they are not 100% foolproof. Specifically, any brand new scam will usually take some time before it is blocked by this type of security service.

If an online or email offer appears too good to be true, it usually is just a ploy to try to get malicious software into your device or take secret information from you.

In one attack, cyber criminals even got into the email system of a lawyers practice and sent what appeared to be a legitimate email asking for the payment for a house to be made to a new account. So – especially with any high value transaction, never confirm information only through email. Make direct contact to help ensure the request is legitimate.

Expect that high value transactions are particularly attractive targets for criminals.

Cyber criminals are also using text messages to perform scams. This technique is known as *smishing*. Just like the email scams, if you receive any unsolicited text messages urgently requiring you to call a number, reply or visit a website – the chances are high that it is just a scam.

…and those cyber criminals will even go as far as sending out very legitimate looking physical mail through the post. Again, this form of scam seeks to get you to call a number, visit a website or send details by any other means.

The simple rule is not to trust any websites or messages of any type that you were not expecting.

Phone scams – 'vishing'

One of the most underhand types of attacks uses phone calls. By calling a victim, the criminals again seek to extract information, record your voice for future fraud attempts and / or get the person to visit a site and unwittingly install malicious software. This form of attack is known as *vishing*, a combination of the words **v**oice and ph**ishing**.

If you receive an unsolicited call and anything seems in the least bit suspicious – end the call. It is also worthwhile reporting it to whatever organization the call pretended to come from, taking care to only use a number that you know is genuine.

If you do call an organization back to authenticate their identity, you also need to do it from a phone that is on a different number from the one they called you on. A frequent vishing trick is for the caller to convince you of their identity by suggesting you call them back on a number you know to be genuine, such as the number on the back of your credit card. If you use the same phone they called you on, they simply stay on the line. Even though they make it sound like you dialed them, in fact you are still on the original call.

Never reveal information, never respond to a request to visit a specific site and never open any file on the instruction of an unknown and unverified caller.

Recognizing pressure

Many of these scams rely on making you think there is some time pressure to perform the action they are requesting. So any time you feel that you are being pressured to do something, take it as an indicator that the person making the request is actually trying to scam you.

Social engineering

Sadly, the most lucrative scams can take substantial amounts from their victims by building up trust over a period of time. Social engineering is the act of a cyber criminal or other hostile person building your trust or confidence in them so they can use that trust to get you to do something for them.

These criminals hang out on social media platforms, dating websites and even in real places (such as bars and restaurants). They will often research their target; find out their interests and their personal vulnerabilities and even their level of personal wealth. They will then use that information to optimize their attack.

As an example, a lonely person might find a perfect online match that is (in reality) a fake profile. They may correspond with that person for some time, gradually disclosing more and more information about themselves. In some cases, the criminal then fakes experiencing some personal financial difficulty and requests or accepts money from their victim.

This type of attack happens regularly.

So remember - as security in our technology improves, cyber criminals know that it can be easier to persuade the legitimate owner to use their valid credentials to make a transaction for them through a confidence trick.

What is 'being pwned'?

To be '*pwned*' in the context of cybersecurity is when you have some of your confidential account details stolen. You can find a fuller definition at the back of the book.

There is also a further FREE online resource that collects copies from some of the largest breaches of stolen information. It can identify if a username or email you use appears on the lists it holds. Be aware though that you are disclosing part of your information to this service in order to use it. You can find that service here:

https://haveibeenpwned.com/

As at March 2017, the service is being run by respected security expert @TroyHunt

Is Online Anonymity Achievable?

It is often reported that there are ways to maintain almost complete anonymity online. That is in fact very hard to do. It is possible – but much harder than many think.

In this section, we provide a very brief outline of what people who try to completely contain their anonymity typically do. If you have a deep interest in achieving advanced anonymity, you will need to read around this subject and be willing to evolve your understanding of technology much further than is covered in this short section.

Achieving anonymity is an advanced skill and the steps required are constantly evolving.

Even when people with very sophisticated technical knowledge think they have done everything to make a set of their online activities anonymous, they often still leave traces of their identity without even knowing it.

It is always much better to consider that any attempts at anonymity will have gaps and that if someone really wants to identify who you are they will be able to.

A great example of this is with email. You may be able to set-up what you think is a very secure, encrypted email account – but there are so many strands of information to hide that a message you think is completely anonymous is likely to have multiple clues as to the identity of its sender.

- You CAN put tape over any camera built in to a device.

- You can also try to smother any built-in microphone.

- You can run all of your information using a VPN service (virtual private network) to help mask your location.

- There is even a special browser called TOR (the onion router) that can be obtained free and helps to hide your identity - Although beware of where you get it from, as some versions will be loaded with their own malware!

- You can set-up a covert, anonymous email address with encryption security.

Even if you do all of these things, there are still hundreds of potential minor slip-ups that mean that a motivated investigator can still find out who you are and where you are.

However, it would be much harder and more expensive for someone running these (and other) anonymity measures to be identified.

A more practical route for most people is to be very careful about what you choose to put online. You may not have complete anonymity – but the more information you choose to put online, especially on public Internet view, the higher your chances of being targeted.

Cyber criminals have tools that can scan and gather publicly available email addresses and other information posted on social media services such as Facebook and LinkedIn.

There are also some FREE (and some paid) software options such as *privacy badger* and *ghostery* that can be installed on some Internet browsers. These can help to reduce (but not completely eliminate) the amount of tracking and information that your browser shares as your surf the Internet. (Remember to only download these from trusted sources and organizations).

So you can take steps to be as anonymous as possible – but never rely on the fact that they completely mask who you are or where you are.

Epilogue

A bear is chasing two men. One of the men turns to the other and says 'You'll never outrun the bear – stop running', the other replies 'I don't need to outrun the bear. I only need to outrun you.'

It's an old joke – but it has relevance in the world of cybersecurity.

Although cybercrime is at a pandemic level, ALL and I mean ALL of the major attacks on organizations always prove to be due to the absence of 3 or more security measures they should have taken.

For private individuals, the picture is very similar. Although the attacks are smaller scale, the criminals are rarely doing anything other than taking advantage of large gaps in our basic security.

Those cyber criminals know:

- Most people re-use their passwords on other accounts.

- Most passwords are only 8 or 9 characters long.

- Most people operate their computers, tablets and smart phones using an account that has automatic installation privileges.

- Most private people do not (yet) run nextgen anti-malware that blocks >99% of malware.

- Most people do not have devices that have all the latest updates in place.

- Most people do not have a completely protected copy (a back-up) of their critical and valuable information.

- Approximately 1 in 5 of us is likely to fall for scams, when they are clever enough to look like a genuine request.

There are so many people that do not take basic security precautions – that if you take the time to cover the basics and stay alert to potential scams, although your protection will not be 100% perfect, it will be hundreds of times better than most people.

Criminals are generally lazy. They want the easy targets. If you are one of the harder targets, unless you have an extremely high value, they will simply move on and try their luck on the next person.

…and just remember that any payment of ransomware helps to support cybercrime. Never pay ransomware. If you do, your details will be shared and you become even more likely to be targeted again and again.

If you run the right anti-malware, your chances of ransomware are much reduced (but not completely eliminated) – but if you hold a safe (separate) copy of your valuable information, it should always be possible to recover from a ransomware attack without losing information or paying the criminals. A successful ransomware attack will cost you time and *is* likely to cost money – but just make sure you don't provide any of that money to the criminals.

Criminals are mostly opportunists looking for the easy targets. Consider the Internet to be like living in an area with a high crime rate. If you employ all of the fundamental security measures described in this book, you will not be an easy target. You cannot completely eliminate all of the risk – but you can come close to eliminating *nearly* all of the risk.

Cybersecurity to English (Abridged)

This is a shortened version of the publication 'The Cybersecurity to English Dictionary' – the full publication contains a much, much longer list of terms and definitions.

access controls – rules and techniques used to manage and restrict entry to or exit from a physical, virtual or digital area through the use of permissions. Permissions are usually assigned individually to a person, device or **application** service to ensure accountability and traceability of usage. The permissions can be secured using (i) physical tokens (something you have); for example a key card, (ii) secret information (something you know); such as a **password** or (iii) biometric information – using part of the human body such as a fingerprint or eye scan to gain access (something you are). See also **multi-factor authentication**.

administrative access – any electronic account that has the authority to perform elevated activities. An elevated activity is any action that can apply significant changes to one or more **digital devices**, software **applications** or services. For example, the permission to install new software is considered an elevated privilege requiring this elevated authorization level.

Advanced Persistent Threats (APTs) – a term used to describe the tenacious and highly evolved set of tactics used by **hackers** to infiltrate **networks** through **digital devices** and to then leave malicious software in place for as long as possible. The **cyber attack lifecycle** usually involves the **attacker** performing research & reconnaissance, preparing the most effective **attack** tools, getting an initial foothold into the network or the target **digital landscape**, spreading the infection and adjusting the range of attack tools in place to then **exploit** the position to maximum advantage. The purpose can be to steal or corrupt an organization's digital **data** or to extort money from the organization and/or disrupt its operations, for financial gain, brand damage or other political purposes. This form of sophisticated attack becomes harder and more costly to resolve the further into the lifecycle the attackers are and the longer they have managed to already leave the malicious software in place. A goal with this **threat** type is for the intruder to remain (persist) undetected for as long as possible in order to maximize the opportunities presented by the intrusion – for example, to steal **data** over a long period of time. See also **kill-chain**.

adware – any computer program (software) designed to render adverts to an end user. This type of software can be considered a form of **malware** if (i) the advertising was not consented to by the user, (ii) it is made difficult to uninstall or remove, or (iii) it provides other covert malware functions.

air gap – to use some form of physical and electronic separation to ensure that activities in one area cannot impact or infect activities in another. Used in the context of **cybersecurity** to describe how sensitive or infected **systems** are physically and digitally isolated so they have no possibility of interacting with any other systems and **networks**.

anti-malware – is a computer program designed to look for specific files and behaviors (**signatures**) that indicate the presence or the attempted installation of malicious software. If or when detected, the program seeks to isolate the **attack** (**quarantine** or block the **malware**), remove it, if it can, and also alert appropriate people to the attempt or to the presence of the **malware**. The program can be host-based (installed on **devices** that are directly used by people) or network-based (installed on **gateway** devices through which information is passed). Older forms of this software could detect only specific, pre-defined forms of malicious software using **signature** files. Newer forms use **machine learning** and make use of additional techniques including **behavior monitoring**.

anti-spyware – a subset of **anti-malware** software that has the specific purpose of detecting, blocking or preventing the installation or operation of malicious software used to illicitly monitor user behavior, improve ad targeting and sometimes steal information. See also **spyware**.

anti-virus – predecessor of **anti-malware** software that was used before the nature and types of malicious software had diversified. This is a computer program designed to look for the presence or installation of specific files. If or when detected, the program seeks to isolate the **attack** (**quarantine** or block the **virus**), remove it, if it can, and also alert appropriate people to the attempt. A virus is only one form of **malware**, so the term anti-malware is considered to be more inclusive of other forms of malicious software. However, as people are more familiar with the term 'anti-virus,' this can sometimes be used to describe various types of anti-malware. See also **anti-malware** and **virus**.

application – a collection of functions and instructions in electronic format (a software program) that resides across one or more **digital devices**, usually designed to create, modify, process, store, inspect and/or transmit specific types of **data**. For subversive applications, see **malware**.

APT – see **Advanced Persistent Threat.**

artificial intelligence – the development of knowledge and skills in computer programs (**applications**) to the extent that they are able to perform perception, recognition, translation and/or decision-making activities without prior direct experience of the event. See also **singularity**, **digital sentience** and **synthetic intelligence**.

asset – any item (physical or digital) that has inherent value. For

cybersecurity, information items that can be monetized (for example, intellectual property and sets of personal **data**) are regarded as high-value assets due to their potential resale or blackmail value.

asymmetric cryptography – a method of **ciphering** information using two different keys (a **key pair**). One is a **public key**, the other is a **private key**. One key is used to cipher the information from plain text into a secret format. The other key can then be used to decipher the secret format back to plain text. The keys can be used in any order as long as both keys are used. As one key is public, the use of the private key first is usually only for the purpose of attaching a **digital signature**. A single key cannot be used to cipher and decipher the same message (single key use to cipher and decipher information is called **symmetric cryptography**). Also known as **public key encryption** and **public key cryptography**.

attack – the occurrence of an unauthorized intrusion.

attacker – an umbrella term used to cover all types of people and organizations that may attempt to gain unauthorized access to a **digital device, application, system** or **network**. See also **black hat, hacker, hacktivist, cyber warrior, script kiddies...**

attack mechanism – a term that describes the method used to achieve an unauthorized intrusion.

attack method – the technique, tools or **exploit** used by an adversary to attempt to gain unauthorized access to any part of a **digital landscape**.

attack signature – a distinctive pattern of characteristics that can be identified to help understand and correct an attempt at unauthorized access or intrusion. See also **indicators of compromise (IOC)**.

attack vector – a path or means that could be used by an unauthorized party to gain access to a **digital device, network** or **system**.

authentication – the process of confirming whether the identity and other properties of any entity (person or **application**) are valid and genuine.

authorization – the use of **authentication** information together with **access control** lists to verify whether or not an entity (person or **application**) has permission to perform the function they are requesting.

availability – the assignment of a value to a set of information to indicate how much disruption or outage the owner considers to be acceptable. Often this is expressed or translated into a scale of time. **Data** with the highest possible availability rating would be required to be readily accessible at all times (no downtime permitted), often through the use of a fully redundant failsafe. The value assigned to the information's availability is used by the owner of an **application** or service to set the **recovery time objective**. See also **integrity** – a different, but related term.

backup – (i) the process of archiving a copy of something so that it can be restored following a disruption. (ii) having a redundant (secondary) capability to continue a process, service or **application** if the primary capability is disrupted.

Bitcoin – a decentralized, virtual digital currency (**cryptocurrency**) and payment **system**, based on a distributed, public ledger. The currency provides a high degree of transactional anonymity as balances and ledger entries are associated with private cryptographic keys and not with the individual or company that uses the system (lose your key, lose your money). This has made it, along with other digital currencies, a payment method of choice for **cyber criminals**, who also use it to receive cyber blackmail payments. The invention of Bitcoin is also associated with the invention of a sophisticated **encryption**-based authenticity technique known as **blockchain**. See also **blockchain**.

bot – is a computer program designed to perform specific tasks. They are usually simple, small and designed to perform fast, repetitive tasks. When the purpose of the program conflicts with an organization's goals and needs, a bot can be considered to be a form of **malware**. See also **botnet**.

botnet – shortened version of robotic network. A connected set of programs designed to operate together over a **network** (including the Internet) to achieve specific purposes. These purposes can be good or bad. Some programs of this type are used to help support Internet connections, while malicious uses include taking **control** of some or all of a computer's functions to support large-scale service **attacks** (see **denial of service**). A botnet is sometimes referred to as a **zombie army**.

brute force (attack) – the use of a systematic approach that can quickly generate large volumes of possible methods to gain unauthorized access to a computer **system**. For example, an automated script can run through the large but finite number of possibilities to try to guess a given eight-character **password** in a matter of seconds. Computing speeds make brute force attempts to try millions of possibilities easy if other defenses are not present. A common defense against this type of attack is to detect and block more than a few attempts at guessing any security information.

clickbait – enticing content generated by advertisers or criminals that encourages or pressures the recipient, or viewer, to want to access the **URL** link or attached file that is on offer. Originally this term was used to describe methods that advertisers would use to drive traffic to a particular web page; however, it is also a primary technique used to make **phishing**

communications attractive to the unwary recipient.

cloud (the) – an umbrella term used to identify any technology service that uses software and equipment not physically managed or owned by the person or organization (customer) using it. This usually provides the advantage of on-demand scalability at lower cost. Examples include **applications** that are hosted online, online file storage areas, and even remote virtual computers. Using a cloud means the equipment managing the service is run by the cloud provider and not by the customer. But although the customer does not own the service, he or she is still accountable for the information that he or she chooses to store and process through it. Usually a **cloud** service is identified by an 'aaS' suffix. For example – **SaaS** (Software as a Service), **IaaS** (Infrastructure as a Service) and **PaaS** (Platform as a Service).

cloud computing – the use of remote servers hosted on the Internet. The term 'cloud' refers to the user's lack of knowledge about exactly where the processing or actions they are performing are being handled. Often a cloud symbol is used to denote the lack of specific information being made available in a representation. It is also possible to have a **private cloud** not hosted on the Internet. Where that occurs, the term is used to denote a lack of transparency on the exact physical machines where the computing is occurring. However, a private cloud can also be hosted over the Internet using security measures designed to keep the resources exclusive to the customer.

cloud security – a term used to describe the collective **policies,** technologies, **procedures** and other **controls** that are used to protect a technology service hosted by an external organization. Cloud platforms are typically Internet accessible and shared with many customers, requiring stronger security than services delivered within an isolated **network** require.

compartmentalization – a security technique that can be

applied to high-value **assets**. The assets can be placed in a more isolated **system**, **network** or **device** requiring additional security **controls** to access. This is designed to add greater protection for those assets. When this is done within a device, it may also be a form of **containerization**.

crack – to break into a secured **digital device**, account or service by defeating one or more security measures designed to prevent the intrusion.

credential stuffing – a high volume form of a **password** re-use **attack**. Due to the large number of people who re-use passwords across different **systems** and **applications**, some criminals leverage usernames and passwords obtained from one source to attempt to gain access to another. This can be accomplished at high volume and high speed using automated tools. Users can prevent this type of attack from being successful simply by always using a unique password. Systems can decrease the chances of this happening when they can detect and block unusual access attempts.

cryptocurrency – any digital currency that makes use of **encryption** to generate and secure confidence in the units that are traded. These forms of payment are usually decentralized and unregulated, and it is difficult to trace currency owners. This makes cryptocurrency the main form of payment for **cybercrime** and **ransomware**. See also **Bitcoin** and **blockchain**.

cryptoviral extortion – the use of a specific form of **malware** that seeks to spread (install in new locations) and **cipher** (**encrypt**) the victim's information for the purpose of demanding payment for the information's release. See also **ransomware**.

cyber attack – an aggressive or hostile action that leverages or targets **digital devices**. The intended damage is not limited to the digital (electronic) environment.

cyber attack lifecycle – a conceptual model of the sequential steps that are involved in a successful unauthorized intrusion or disruption into a **digital landscape** or **digital device**. There are a number of models currently available; an example of the most common steps found across the models are illustrated within the definition of **advanced persistent threat**. See also **kill chain**.

cybercrime – an act that violates the laws of one or more countries through the illicit use of or access to one or more digital technologies.

cyber criminal – any person who attempts to gain unauthorized access to one or more **digital devices**.

cyber defense – the collective set of technologies, processes and people that act to defend any given **digital landscape**.

cybersecurity – the protection of **digital devices** and their communication channels to keep them stable, dependable and reasonably safe from danger or **threat**. Usually the required protection level must be sufficient to prevent or address unauthorized access or intervention before it can lead to substantial personal, professional, organizational, financial and/or political harm. In the UK this term is used as 2 words – **cyber security**.

cyberspace – the area available for electronic information to exist inside any collection of interconnected **digital devices**.

darknet – the emergent term to describe the collection of websites that hide their server locations. Although publicly accessible, they are not registered on standard search engines, and the hidden server values make it extremely difficult to determine which organizations and people are behind these sites.

Previously referred to mainly as the **dark web**, see also **dark Internet** (different meaning in the past).

data – information stored in an electronic or digital format.

data classification – the process of arranging sets of electronic information into categories based on their value, impact, required level of secrecy and other attributes. Typical attributes for this categorization process include **confidentiality**, **integrity** (the need for the information to be uncorrupted) and **availability**.

DDoS – acronym for **Distributed Denial of Service**. See **Denial of Service** for definition.

DDoS filtering – the process security technologies use to sift through any barrage of **data** requests sent as part of an **attack** to identify and allow legitimate traffic to pass, while preventing or limiting the impact of the illegitimate requests. See also **Denial of Service** for information about this attack type.

decapitation – (in the context of **malware**) preventing any compromised **device** from being able to communicate, receive instruction, send information or spread malware to other devices. This can effectively render many forms of malware ineffective because it removes any command, **control** or theft benefit. This is often a stage during **takedown** or **threat** removal.

default accounts – generic user and **password** permissions, often with administrative access that is provided as standard for some **applications** and hardware for use during initial setup.

Denial of Service (DoS) – an **attack** designed to stop or disrupt peoples' use of organizations' **systems**. Usually, a particular section of an enterprise is targeted; for example, a specific **network**, **system**, **digital device** type or function.

These attacks usually originate from, and are targeted at, **devices** accessible through the Internet. If the attack is from multiple source locations, it is referred to as a **Distributed Denial of Service**, or **DDoS** attack.

device encryption – usually refers to encoding (making unreadable) the information at rest on a smartphone, tablet, laptop or other electronic item. This encoding makes the information stored on the item readable only when a valid user is logged in.

devices – any hardware used to create, modify, process, store or transmit **data**. Computers, smartphones and **USB** drives are all examples of devices.

digital device – any electronic appliance that can create, modify, archive, retrieve or transmit information in an electronic format. Desktop computers, laptops, tablets, smartphones and Internet-connected home **devices** are all examples of digital devices.

digital forensics – a specialized field in which personnel help preserve, rebuild and recover electronic information and help investigate and uncover residual evidence after an **attack**. See also **indicators of compromise**.

digital landscape – the collection of **digital devices** and electronic information that is visible or accessible from a particular location.

Distributed Denial of Service (DDoS) – see **Denial of Service**.

distributed guessing – an **attack** technique that allows the jigsaw of information about a person or his or her credit card that is held or accessible across multiple websites to be assembled into enough information to perform a fraudulent transaction. This type of attack takes advantage of (i) the different pieces of available information that may be held on each website service and (ii) the ability to make multiple invalid guesses on each site, with no centralized lockout of the card or the user's personal details. Using this technique through automated tooling, an **attacker** can turn basic information such as 4 card digits and a person's name into complete credit card details, including the long card number, validity dates and security code.

DNS – acronym for **D**omain **N**ame **S**ystem. Whenever a **network** or Internet location uses a plain text name (such as www.cybersimplicity.com), this has to be translated into a specific and more technical location called the **IP address**. A **DNS service** runs on a server to reconcile and translate the text value into the specific network location's IP address value.

doxxing (also **doxing**) – publicly exposing personal information on the Internet. Thought to be based on an abbreviation of the word 'documenting.'

drive-by download – the unintended receipt of malicious software onto a device through an Internet page, electronic service or link. The victim is usually unaware that his or her actions permitted new malicious software to be pulled onto and installed into the **digital device** or **network**.

dwell-time – in the context of **cybersecurity** – this refers to how long an intrusion or **threat** has been allowed to remain in place before being discovered and eliminated. The length of time between intrusion and detection is an indication of how successful an **advanced persistent threat** has been. Although the dwell-time is expected to fall as cybersecurity measures mature, the average time is often hundreds of days and can be years.

encryption – the act of encoding messages so that if they are intercepted by an unauthorized party, they cannot be read unless the encoding mechanism can be deciphered.

endpoint – a final digital destination where electronic information is processed by users. Computers, smartphones and tablet **devices** are all examples of endpoints.

endpoint protection – a term used to describe the collective set of security software that has become standard for most user-operated **digital devices**. The security software may include **anti-malware**, a personal **firewall**, intrusion prevention software and other protective programs and processes.

endpoint security – see **endpoint protection**.

exfiltrate – to move something with a degree of secrecy sufficient to not be noticed. Used to describe moving stolen **data** through detection **systems**.

exploit – to take advantage of a security **vulnerability**. Well-known exploits are often given names. Falling victim to a known exploit with a name can be a sign of low security, such as poor **patch management**.

exploited – see **exploit**.

fake website – can either be (i) a fraudulent imitation of a real Internet page or site designed to look like one from the legitimate company, or (ii) an Internet page or site from a completely fake company, often with a 'too good to be true' offer or misleading content. In both instances, the objectives of the site may include capturing genuine log-in credentials, receiving real payments for orders that will not be delivered, or installing **malware**.

firewall – is hardware (physical device) or software (computer program) used to monitor and protect inbound and outbound **data** (electronic information). It achieves this by applying a set of rules. These physical **devices** or computer programs are usually deployed, at a minimum, at the perimeter of each **network** access point. Software firewalls can also be deployed on devices to add further security. The rules applied within a firewall are known as the **firewall policy**. Advanced firewalls are often equipped with other defensive features typical of more **unified threat management**.

firewall policy – the rules applied within either a physical hardware **device** (a hardware **firewall**) or software program (a software firewall) to allow or block specific types of inbound and outbound **data** traffic at the perimeter of a **network** or **digital device**.

hack – the act of gaining unauthorized access to a **digital device**, **network**, **system**, account or other electronic **data** repository.

hacker – a person who engages in attempts to gain unauthorized access to one or more **digital devices**. Can be **black hat** (unethical) or **white hat** (ethical) hacker, depending on the person's intent.

hacktivism – an amalgamation of **hacker** and activism. Describes the act of seeking unauthorized access into any **digital device** or **digital landscape** to promote a social or political agenda. Usually the unauthorized access is used to cause destruction, disruption and/or publicity. Individuals participating in these acts are called **hacktivists**.

hacktivist – an amalgamation of the words **hacker** and activist. Describes any individual who participates in **hacktivism**.

hashing – using a mathematical function to convert any block or group of **data** into a fixed-length value (usually shorter than the original data) that represents the original data. This fixed-length value can be used for fast indexing of large files by computer programs without the need to manage the larger data block. It is also used extensively in the field of security; for example, **digital forensics** can use this technique to verify that the data content of a copy of any examined data is identical to the original source.

incident response – a prepared set of processes that should be triggered when any known or suspected event takes place that could cause material damage to an organization. The typical stages are (i) verify the event is real and identify the affected areas, (ii) contain the problem (usually by isolating, disabling or disconnecting the affected pieces), (iii) understand and eradicate the root cause, (iv) restore the affected components to their fixed state and (v) review how the process went to identify improvements that should be made. An incident response may also be required to trigger other response **procedures**, such as a **breach notification procedure**, if there is any information which has been lost that is subject to a notification requirement. For example, the loss of any personal information beyond what might be found in a phone book entry is usually considered to be a notifiable event.

indicators of compromise (IOC) – is a term originally used in computer **forensics** to describe any observable behaviors and patterns (such as particular blocks of **data**, registry changes, **IP address** references) that strongly suggest that a computer intrusion has occurred or is taking place. The collation of these patterns and behaviors are now actively used in **advanced threat defense** to help more rapidly identify potential security issues from across a monitored **digital landscape**.

infection – (in the context of **cybersecurity**), unwanted invasion by an outside agent that an **attacker** uses to create damage or disruption.

Internet of Things (IoT) – the incorporation of electronics into everyday items sufficient to allow them to **network** (communicate) with other network-capable **devices**. For example, to include electronics in a home thermostat so that it can be operated and can share information over a network connection to a smartphone or other network-capable device.

Internet Protocol – is the set of rules used to send or receive information from or to a location on a **network**, including information about the source, destination and route. Each electronic location (host) has a unique address (the **IP address**) that is used to define the source and the destination.

Intrusion Detection and Prevention Systems (IDPS) – computer programs that monitor and inspect electronic communications that pass through them, with the purpose and ability (i) to block and log (record) key information about any known malicious or otherwise unwanted streams of information and (ii) to log and raise alerts about any other traffic that is suspected (but not confirmed) to be of a similar nature. These are usually placed in the communication path to allow the IDPS to prevent unwanted information from entering or leaving a **network** by dropping or blocking **packets**. IDPS can also clean some electronic **data** to remove any unwanted or undesirable packet components.

IoT – see **Internet of Things**.

least privilege – a basic security access practice of granting each person or user account the minimum amount of **access rights** required to perform their role.

MAC address – abbreviation for media access control **address**. This is a unique identifier assigned to every single **digital device** with a **network** interface controller. If a device has multiple controllers, it may have multiple (unique) addresses, one for each controller. If the identifier (MAC address) is assigned by the manufacturer, part of it will include the manufacturer's identification number. There are several related format conventions in existence. The identifier is used in network (including Internet) communications.

macro virus – a form of malicious software designed to operate from within files used by other (usually legitimately installed) programs. For example, a word processing or spreadsheet file can contain sets of malicious instructions, and, if opened, these instructions will be run by the word processing or spreadsheet software. This bypasses the opportunity for **anti-malware** to detect any new software installation, as the macro virus is leveraging and subverting an **application** that is already in place.

MAC spoofing – impersonating the unique identifier (**MAC address**) of another **network** interface controller.

malware – shortened version of **ma**licious soft**ware**. A term used to describe disruptive, subversive or hostile programs that can be inserted onto a **digital device**. People can intentionally or unintentionally make these types of programs harmful. Intentionally-harmful versions are usually disguised or embedded in a file that looks harmless so the **attacker** who uses them can intentionally compromise a device. Malware that someone does not intend to be harmful can still disrupt a device or leak information; however, the harmful qualities can result from unintentionally poor construction quality, bad design or insecure configuration. There are many types of malware; **adware, botnets, computer viruses, ransomware, scareware, spyware, trojans** and **worms** are all examples of intentional malware. **Hackers** often use malware to mount **cybersecurity attacks**.

man-in-the-browser – a form of **malware attack** that modifies transactions within the **web browser** of the machine it is hosted on, so that covert additional transactions or transaction content can be modified without the victim's knowledge or consent.

man-in-the-middle – the interception and relay by a third party of selected content between two legitimate parties, for the purpose of hijacking or adjusting an electronic transaction. For example, party 1 believes he or she has connected to his or her banking home page, but is actually viewing an emulated screen offered by the intercepting **attacker**. As the login information is provided, the attacker can set up a separate connection to the bank (party 2), and is then able to respond to any challenge made by the bank by passing the same challenge back to the user (party 1). Once authorized in the transaction **system**, the attacker can then make transactions that have not been sanctioned by the user, without the user's immediate knowledge.

man-in-the-mobile – a form of **malware** for mobile phones that steals information and credentials.

master boot record – the first sector on any electronic **device** that defines which **operating system** should be loaded when it is initialized or re-started.

megabreach – when the result of a **cyber attack** involves such a high level of catastrophic theft and/or such extensive intrusion that it leads to worldwide press exposure. As the frequency and scale of breaches have increased, the threshold for newsworthy events has also increased.

metamorphic malware – a more sophisticated form of **malware** that changes all key parts of its code on each installation. **Polymorphic malware** uses fewer transformation techniques than this type of (metamorphic) malware does, as polymorphic malware usually only changes some key parts of its profile, but retains the same core virus. See also **blended threat**.

Mirai – the first of a new type of **botnet malware** that targeted non-secure Internet of Things (**IoT**) devices that shipped with hard-coded usernames and passwords. The malware could be easily added to the non-secure **digital devices** to form an army that hackers could use to perform new scales of Distributed

Denial of Service (**DDoS**) attacks. See also **botnet**.

multi-factor authentication – using more than one form of proof to confirm the identity of a person or **device** attempting to request access. There are usually three different categories of **authentication** types: (i) something you know [often a **password**] (ii) something you have [perhaps a security token or access card] and (iii) something you are [the use of biometrics; for example fingerprint or facial recognition]. As an example, effective two-factor authentication would require that when access is being requested, proof would be required from at least two different categories.

nagware – a form of software that persistently reminds the user that he or she should do something, even though he or she might not want to. This is not usually considered to be malicious software, but it does exhibit some unwanted features that disrupt the flow of the user's interaction with his or her device. Nagware is often used as partial payment for some forms of software, especially free software.

NAS – acronym for **network**-attached storage. A digital repository attached to a **network** where information can be stored.

network – a collective group of **devices**, wiring and **applications** used to connect, carry, broadcast, monitor or safeguard **data**. Networks can be physical (use material **assets** such as wiring) or virtual (use applications to create associations and connections between devices or applications). Usually, the devices on a network will have some form of trusted permissions that allow them to pass and share **packets** of electronic information.

network-based – describes a situation where something is installed to protect, serve or subvert the community of devices, wiring and **applications** used to connect, carry, broadcast, monitor or safeguard information (the **network**).

non-repudiation – the act of ensuring that a user's electronic activity has sufficient identity checks and **audit** evidence in place so that it cannot be refuted or denied by the person performing the action.

open source – an **application**, other computer program or software building block for which the software code is made publicly available for expansion, use or modification by anybody. This makes it very cheap to use, but also opens up a greater potential for malicious subversion, especially if subverted versions of the work are incorporated into **systems** that are intended to be secure.

operating system – the central, low-level software **application** program in any **digital device** that enables the hardware (screen, buttons, etc) to interact with any installed software.

password – a secret string of characters (letters, numbers and other special characters) that can be used to gain entry to a **digital device**, **application** or other service.

patch management – a controlled process used to deploy critical, interim updates to software on **digital devices**. The release of a software 'patch' is usually in response to a critical flaw or gap that has been identified. Any failure to apply new interim software updates promptly can leave open security **vulnerabilities** in place. As a consequence, promptly applying these updates (patch management) is considered a critical component of maintaining effective **cybersecurity**.

payload – the part of the **data** in a transmission that constitutes the usable content rather than the packaging (the cargo). In the context of **cybersecurity**, this term is often used to refer to the harmful data (**malware**, for example) that an **attacker** may attempt to install into a target **digital device network**, or

system. For example, an attacker **exploits** a **vulnerability** to deliver his or her payload of malware.

penetration – (in the context of **cybersecurity**) – intrusion.

penetration test (also known as an **attack and penetration test** or **pen. test**) – checks and scans on any **application**, **system** or website to identify any potential security gaps (**vulnerabilities**) that could be **exploited**. Once the vulnerabilities are identified, this process then goes on to identify the extent to which these vulnerabilities could be leveraged in an attack (the penetration possibilities). Usually these checks are performed in a test area and emulate the same techniques that could be used by an **attacker**. This is to prevent any inadvertent operational disruption. The checks are typically conducted before any application or site is first used, and also on a periodic (repeating) basis; for example, each time the program is updated or every 6 months. Any significant gaps must be addressed (fixed) in a timeframe appropriate to the scale of the **risk**. Not to be confused with the term **vulnerability assessment**, which only identifies gaps without examining how they could be leveraged. See also **pivoting**.

persistence – to seek continued existence despite opposition.

personally identifiable information (PII) – any combination of information that can directly or indirectly distinguish (identify) who a specific individual is.

phishing – using an electronic communication (for example email or instant messaging) that pretends to come from a legitimate source, in an attempt to get sensitive information (for example, a **password** or credit card number) from the recipient or to install **malware** on the recipient's **device**. The methods of phishing have evolved so that the message can simply contain a link to an Internet location where malware is situated or can include an attachment (such as a PDF or Word document) that installs malware when opened. The malware can then be used to run any number of unauthorized functions, including stealing information from the device, replicating additional malware to other accessible locations, sharing the user screen and logging keyboard entries made by the user. Less complex forms of phishing can encourage the recipient to visit a fake but convincing version of a website and to disclose passwords or other details.

physical security – measures designed to deter, prevent, detect or alert unauthorized real-world access to a site or material item.

PII – see **personally identifiable information**.

polymorphic malware – malicious software that can change its attributes to help avoid detection by **anti-malware**. This mutation process can be automated so that the function of the software continues, but the method of operation, location and other attributes may change. See also **metamorphic malware** and **blended threat**.

pop a shell – the act of breaking into the **operating system** or command level **control** system (**shell**) of a computing **device**.

port – a connection point (real or virtual) that helps in the transmission of electronic **data** between electronic **devices** and computer programs. Assigning a specific value (a **port number**) when sending information lets the receiver know what type of information is being sent and how it should be processed. This information can also be used by security devices such as **firewalls** to help allow or deny certain communication types.

privileged account – an electronic user access right that has elevated permissions to allow it to perform **system**, **application**, database or other **digital landscape** management functions. Usually, this form of access requires additional **controls** and supervision to ensure the elevated privileges are fully accountable and are not misused. Most forms of **cyber attack** seek to gain this form of access, as these types of accounts have control over their digital landscape.

proxy server – is a program used to provide intermediate services between a requested transaction and its destination. Instead of sending the transaction 'as is' it can adjust some of the information to help secure the anonymity of the sender. In addition, it may store (cache) any information that is accessed often to help speed up response times.

public – (in the context of **cybersecurity**) indicates that the artifact used in any prefix or suffix is openly available and accessible over the Internet.

pwned – domination or humiliation of a rival, originating from video game play but also applied to **cybersecurity attacks**.

ransomware – a form of malicious software (**malware**) that prevents or restricts usage of one or more **digital devices** or **applications** or renders a collection of electronic **data** unreadable until a sum of money is paid. **Cryptoviral extortion** is an example of the techniques used to perform this type of **attack**.

resilience – the ability to remain functional and capable in the face of **threat** or danger, or to return to function rapidly following any disruption.

risk – a situation involving exposure to significant impact or loss. In formal frameworks, risk can be quantified using probability (often expressed as a percentage) and impact (often expressed as a financial amount). Other parameters for risk can include proximity (how soon a potential risk may be encountered, and information about which **assets**, services, products and processes could be affected).

risk assessment – a systematic process for the proactive detection of potential hazards or gaps in an existing or planned activity, **asset**, service, **application, system** or product.

risk-based – an approach that considers the financial impact of a failure, along with its probability and proximity, to determine its comparative significance and priority for treatment.

rootkit – a set of software tools that can be used by **attackers** to gain privileged access and **control** of the core (root) of the target **device**, where commands can be more easily run. Part of the function of a rootkit usually includes hiding malicious files and processes to help avoid detection and removal of the **malware**.

router – a device used to define the path for **data packets** (electronic information) to follow when they flow between **networks**.

scareware – malicious software that is designed to persuade people to buy an antidote for a computer infection. It usually masquerades as a commercial **malware** removal tool or **anti-virus** package, but in reality is provided by the **attacker**.

script kiddies – an **attacker** with little to no coding (programming) or technical skills who makes use of available scripts, codes and packages to gain unauthorized access to **digital devices, applications, systems** and/or **networks**. Also known as **script bunnies** and **skiddies**.

secure configuration – ensuring that when settings are applied to any item (**device** or software), appropriate steps are always taken to ensure (i) **default accounts** are removed or disabled, (ii) shared accounts are not used and (iii) all protective and defensive **controls** in the item use the strongest appropriate setting(s).

security misconfiguration – one of the **OWASP** top 10 critical security flaws to guard against. To fail to adequately apply security settings or up-to-date security patches to any component in a **digital landscape** or specific software program.

session management – when a person or digital service interacts to and fro with another piece of software or web-based service without interruption, the transactions are considered to be part of one related set of activities between the two parties (a session). To retain continuity and avoid the need for repeated **authentication**, software has to adequately recognize when activities are part of an existing session, or when an activity is part of a new session, requiring new authentication. The process of managing these interactions without the need for re-authentication is known as session management.

shell access – command level permission to perform executive control over an electronic device.

signatures – (in the context of **cybersecurity**) are the unique attributes – for example, file size, file extension, **data** usage patterns and method of operation – that identify a specific computer program. Traditional **anti-malware** and other security technologies can make use of this information to identify and manage some forms of rogue software or communications.

smishing – a **phishing attack** that uses the simple message service (SMS) to send a malicious link or file to a phone as a text message. If the malicious link or attachment is opened, the **device** may be compromised. This form of attack can also use the MMS (multi-media service).

sniffing – the act of monitoring and analyzing traffic to identify and resolve problems in a **network** (network sniffer), **data packet** (packet sniffer) or other level (for example, wireless sniffer).

social engineering – The act of constructing relationships, friendships or other human interactions for the purpose of enticing the recipient to perform an action or reveal information. The individual(s) doing the social engineering use the victim's action or information for the hidden purpose of achieving a nefarious objective, such as acquiring intelligence about the security, location or **vulnerability** of **assets**, or even gaining the person's trust to open an Internet link or document that will result in a **malware** foothold being created.

spear phishing – a more targeted form of **phishing**. This term describes the use of an electronic communication (for example, email or instant messaging) that targets a particular person or group of people (for example, employees at a location) and pretends to come from a legitimate source. In this case, the source may also pretend to be someone known and trusted to the recipient, in an attempt to obtain sensitive information (for example, a **password** or credit card number).

spoofing – concealing the true source of electronic information by impersonation or other means. Often used to bypass Internet security filters by pretending the source is from a trusted location.

spyware – a form of **malware** that covertly gathers and transmits information from the **device** on which it is installed.

SSID – acronym for Service Set Identifier. This is the set of up to 32 characters that are used to recognize a particular Wireless Local Area Network (WLAN) connection on Wi-Fi **routers** and other access points. A list of the values can be seen when any **device** scans for visible wireless connections.

SSL – is an acronym for Secure Sockets Layer. This is a method (**protocol**) for providing **encrypted** communication between two points in a **digital landscape**. For example, this could be between a **web server** (the computer hosting a web service or web site) and a **web browser** (the program that the recipient uses to view the web page; for example, Internet Explorer). In the **URL** (the Internet address visible to the user), the use of SSL is denoted by an 'https:' prefix.

sucker list – an identified set of soft targets that are easy to take advantage of due to their propensity to pay **ransomware** demands and/or to have a weak security position.

systems – groups of **applications** that operate together to serve a more complex purpose.

threat – any source of potential harm to the **digital landscape**.

threat actors – an umbrella term to describe the collection of people and organizations that work to create **cyber attacks**. Examples of threat actors can include **cyber criminals**, **hacktivists** and nation states.

threat intelligence – the collation of information about potential hostile actions that could occur, together with an understanding of their relative probabilities.

threat landscape – see **threatscape**.

threatscape – a term that amalgamates **threat** and landscape. An umbrella term to describe the overall, expected methods (**vectors**) and types of **cyber attackers** through or by which an organization or individual might expect to be attacked.

TOR – is a free software **application** designed to protect the anonymity of the people who use it. The name is an acronym for 'The Onion Router,' the project from which the application evolved and a reference to how the software operates. Communications use multiple layers of **encryption** that enable them to travel through multiple locations without ever revealing both the originator and destination in any single step. At each step during the relay of the communication, only a single layer of the transmission route is revealed, with all remaining layers remaining encrypted. The final **IP address** destination is only revealed in the very last layer. The originating IP address of the communication is not revealed during any part of the communication relay, other than during the very first part of the relay. This mechanism is used to facilitate anonymous access to resources like the **darknet**.

trojan – an **application** (software program) that appears to be harmless, but that actually hides and facilitates the operation of other, unseen malicious and unauthorized software programs and activities.

trusted network – an area of interconnected **digital devices** in which the security **controls** and the assignment of authorizations and privileges are subject to a known and acceptable level of control. The opposite of an **untrusted network**.

two-factor authentication – see **multi-factor authentication**.

typosquatting – part of a method of **attack** where the perpetrator acquires a domain name that looks at first glance to belong to a major organization. Attacks that leverage an incorrectly spelt domain are used in some forms of **phishing** and other attacks.

unauthorized access – to gain entry without permission.

Unified Threat Management (UTM) – a security **device** that integrates a large number of security technologies and services. For example, a single **gateway** device that includes proxy **firewall**, **intrusion prevention**, gateway **anti-malware** and **VPN** functions.

untrusted network – an area of interconnected **digital devices** in which the security **controls** and/or assignment of authorizations and privileges are not subject to any centralized or acceptable level of control.

URL – acronym for **u**niform **r**esource **l**ocator. This is essentially the address (or path) where a particular destination can be found. For example, the main address for the Google website is the URL http://www.google.com

USB – acronym for **U**niversal **S**erial **B**us. This is a standard connector that exists on most computers, smartphones, tablets and other physical electronic **devices** that allow other electronic devices to be connected. Used for attaching a range of devices including keyboards, mice, external displays, printers and external storage devices.

vector – another word for 'method,' as in 'They used multiple vectors for the **attack**.'

virtual desktop – a **virtual machine** that emulates the functions of a personal computer. See **virtual machine**.

virtual machine – a computer with an **operating system** that can run **applications** but that does not physically exist. Instead of running on an exclusive piece of physical hardware, the computer is merely a set of software and configuration files. Multiple virtual machines can exist on a single physical machine, or a single virtual machine can exist across multiple physical machines through the use of a **hypervisor**. Virtual machines are often used for security purposes, as they are quick to clean, easy to set up and useful for isolating **threats**.

virtual private network (VPN) – a method of providing a secure connection between two points over a public (or unsecure) infrastructure; for example, to set up a secure link between a remote company laptop in a hotel and the main company **network**.

virtual reality – a fully artificial, computer-generated simulation of a real environment. See also **augmented reality**.

virus – a form of **malware** that spreads by infecting (attaching itself to) other files and that usually seeks opportunities to continue this pattern. Viruses are now less common than other forms of malware, but were the main type of malware in very early computing. For that reason, people often refer to something as a virus when it is technically another form of malware.

vishing – abbreviation for voice ph**ishing**. The use of a phone call or similar communication method (such as instant messaging) where the caller attempts to deceive the recipient into performing an action (such as visiting a **URL**), or into revealing information that can then be used to obtain unauthorized access to **systems** or accounts. Usually, the ultimate purpose is to steal (or hold ransom) something of value. These types of calls are becoming extremely prevalent, as the criminal gangs involved may have already stolen part of the recipient's **data** (name, phone number...) to help persuade the person receiving the call that it is authentic and legitimate. As a rule, if you did not initiate a call or message, you should never comply with any demand, especially to visit any webpage or link.

vulnerabilities – **see vulnerability**.

vulnerability – (in the context of **cybersecurity**) a weakness, usually in design, implementation or operation of software (including **operating systems**), that could be compromised and result in damage or harm.

water holing – a method of **cyber attack** that identifies a location where a group of targets are known to visit frequently for the purpose of infecting them with **malware**.

web browser – the program a person uses on his or her **device** to view a web page. Examples of web browser programs include

Internet Explorer and Firefox.

web server – is a computer that is used to host (provide) a web service or web site.

worm – a form of malicious software (**malware**) that seeks to find other locations to which it can replicate. This helps to both protect the malware from removal and to increase the area of the **attack surface** that is compromised.

zero-day – refers to the very first time a new type of **exploit** or new piece of **malware** is discovered. At that point in time, none of the **anti-virus**, **anti-malware** or other defenses may be set up to defend against the new form of exploit.

I